THE SAUCE THAT WENT BANG!

Written by Abie Longstaff

Illustrated by Diego Funck

Collins

It was a normal day. It was an ordinary lunchtime.
But life was about to change forever …

Mum and Dad and Josh and Zena were sitting at
the kitchen table.

"Don't play with your lettuce, Zena," said Mum.

"What's wrong with your carrots, Josh?" said Dad.
"Eat up!"

Josh sighed and put down his fork. "These carrots
are so … boring," he said. "They just taste of carrot."

"Yeah," Zena grumbled. "And this lettuce isn't …
special. It only tastes of … lettuce."

"Wait a minute – " Josh leapt onto his chair. "Let's make something!" he declared.

"Yes!" cried Zena, climbing up to join him. "Something to make food taste special."

"No longer will carrots taste of carrot," announced Josh.

"No more will lettuce taste of lettuce," proclaimed Zena.

Josh and Zena poured and mixed and shook
and stirred. They added sweet things and wet things,
crunchy things and soft things, and hot things and
cold things. But the mixture didn't taste special.

"It needs to dance on the lips!" said Josh.

"It should zing on the tongue!" cried Zena.

"We want a flavour that explodes in the mouth!"
they insisted.

4

They added:

jumping beans for dancing,

nettle for zing,

popcorn for KA-POW!!

They tasted it ...

It danced! It zinged! It exploded in the mouth!

Josh and Zena looked at each other in glee. They had invented a sauce! The best sauce in the world.

"All food will taste of this sauce," they promised. "All food will be special!"

They called it:

Special Sauce™.

From that day on, the family had Special Sauce™
with everything they ate. Mum poured it on eggs.
Josh and Zena put it in sandwiches. And Dad served it
to guests with pride. Soon all the kids at school and all
the neighbours in the street wanted Special Sauce™.

6

Josh and Zena were super busy. They worked in
the mornings before school, and in the evenings after
school, and Saturdays and Sundays.

"We can't keep up with the demand!" said Josh,
swaying with exhaustion.

"Our sauce is so popular," gasped Zena, her fingers
aching from screwing caps onto bottles.

Mum and Dad left their jobs to help. Mum bought
the ingredients, Dad mixed them up, Zena poured
the sauce into bottles, and Josh sold the bottles in
the front yard.

SPECIAL
SAUCE™

THE FLAVOUR
THAT EXPLODES
IN YOUR MOUTH!

Word spread, and soon the whole town ... the whole country ... the whole *world* demanded Special Sauce™.

Bottles were on the tables in all the restaurants and all the cafés. Supermarkets stocked Special Sauce™ ice-cream and Special Sauce™ cereal, Special Sauce™ pet food and even Special Sauce™ toothpaste.

Every family on the planet happily covered their breakfast, lunch and dinner in Special Sauce™. Now all food tasted only of Special Sauce™.

9

Josh and Zena opened an enormous Special Sauce™ factory so they could make gazillions of bottles of sauce, and fly them round the globe.

Soon, Zena and Josh were rich and famous! They had fancy bikes and swanky coats and a treehouse with its own swimming pool.

Mum had a feathered hat, and Dad had sparkly
shoes, and even Tiddles, their cat, had a diamond collar.

This could be the end of the story. The family could
live happily ever after. You can stop reading now, if
you like.

Do you want to carry on? Are you sure? OK then …

It was a (new) normal day. It was an ordinary
(Special Sauce™) lunchtime. But life was about to
change forever (again) …

Mum and Dad and Josh and Zena were sitting at
the (really expensive) kitchen table.

"Have some Special Sauce™ for your lettuce, Zena,"
said Mum.

"Dip those carrots right in, Josh," said Dad.

The sun shone through the window.

"Phew," said Josh. "It's so hot today."

Zena wiped her brow.

The sun shone brighter and brighter, stronger and stronger.

Suddenly, they heard a noise coming from their enormous Special Sauce™ factory next door. It was the sound of bottles dancing, bottles zinging, bottles *exploding*.

Ka-pow!

They ran into the factory. A mess of glass and sauce met their eyes. The bottles of Special Sauce™ Batch Number One had burst!

13

"What's gone wrong?" said Josh.

"I don't understand," said Zena, frowning.

"Our sauce dances on the lips," said Josh.

"It zings on the tongue," said Zena.

"It explodes in the mouth," they said together.

Then they realised: Special Sauce™ didn't only explode in the mouth … it exploded in the bottle too.

"Oh no!" cried Josh.

"What should we do?" asked Zena.

They looked at each other.

"If we tell everyone – " began Josh, his face pale.

"Then we won't be rich," finished Zena. There was a hard knot in her stomach. "We'll have to give up our bikes and our coats and our swimming pool."

"We do like that swimming pool," Josh pointed out. He nibbled his thumbnail.

Tiddles wandered into the factory. She found her favourite patch of sun, just by the bottles of Batch Number Two.

The bottles danced. Rumble, rumble! They zinged. Ting, ting! The bottles …

"Tiddles!" cried Josh. "Watch out!"

Zena scooped her up just before …

… Ka-boom!

Batch Number Two exploded.

Josh and Zena ran into the street.

"Stop!" they cried. "Get rid of your Special Sauce™!"

"No way," the people replied. "We love it too much!"

Just then there was a low rumble. It grew louder and louder until ...

... Bang!

Around the world, Batch Number Three of Special Sauce™ exploded. Then batch four, then batches five, six and seven.

Soon the whole planet was covered in Special Sauce™.

There was sauce on Big Ben, sauce on the Eiffel Tower, sauce on the Statue of Liberty, sauce on the Great Wall and sauce on the Taj Mahal. There was sauce in the park, sauce in the library, sauce in the rivers and sauce on the mountains.

And now, finally, the world had had enough of Special Sauce™.

"I can't bear to look at it!" people complained.

"I can't bear to smell it!" they cried.

"I can't bear to taste it!" they moaned.

Josh and Zena organised a gigantic clean-up day.
Everyone scrubbed and washed and wiped until
the planet was so clean it sparkled. They swept all
the sauce into a huge field.

Then the World Space Agency shot it to the sun.
Fizzzzz went the last traces of Special Sauce™ … bang!

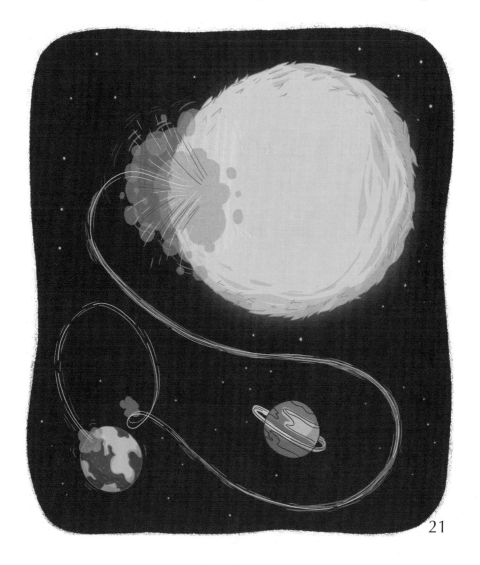

"I'm glad the world is safe," said Josh. "But … now I don't have anything to do." He lay back on the sofa, staring at the ceiling, twiddling his thumbs.

"I'm pleased the world is clean," said Zena. She flicked through the television channels aimlessly. "But the days do feel awfully long."

"Just rest," said Dad. "For a while you two brought a lot of happiness into the world."

"We're so proud of you," said Mum.

At dinner, Josh ate a carrot. "Oh!" he said, in surprise. "I'd forgotten the sweet and smoky taste of carrot. Our Special Sauce™ made all foods taste the same."

Zena crunched on lettuce. "This is so fresh and buttery!" she exclaimed. "I didn't notice that when it was covered in Special Sauce™."

"Maybe it's for the best that our sauce exploded," said Josh. He sat back in his chair.

"Yes," said Zena. "Maybe it's good that everybody can taste their food just as it is." She smiled at her brother.

But people kept knocking on Josh and Zena's door.

"What are we going to put on our food now?" the people asked.

"Can you make us a different sauce?" they wanted to know.

Josh and Zena shook their heads. "We're not going to make a sauce," they said. "It makes everything taste the same. Nothing is sweet or spicy or salty or tangy when it's covered in sauce."

Josh brought out a giant tray of vegetables.

"I think we should try food *without* sauce,"
Zena declared.

There was a hush.

"Please – " said Josh.

"Just try it – " pleaded Zena.

"Only three mouthfuls – " begged Josh, holding out
some broccoli.

"Here comes the train – " Zena jiggled a spoonful of
peas in encouragement.

A little girl stepped up to Josh, her mouth opened wide. She took a big bite of broccoli.

"Mmm," she said, "crunchy and peppery."

"Mmm," said a baby, as he gobbled up the peas.

Soon everyone was eating ... without Special Sauce™. The food tasted delicious and very, very special.

"Our work here is done," said Josh.

Zena nodded and took a sip of water.

"Hmm," she said. "Water is a bit boring."

Josh looked at Zena. Zena looked at Josh.

"Wait a minute!"

"Here they go again," said Mum and Dad, as Josh and Zena rushed into the kitchen.

Should we tell everyone that Special Sauce™ explodes?

If we tell

NO SPECIAL SAUCE

HERE

NEWS

SPECIAL SAUCE BUSINESS FAILS

If we don't tell

Ideas for reading

Written by Gill Matthews
Primary Literacy Consultant

Reading objectives:

- Check that the text makes sense, discuss understanding and explain the meaning of words in context
- Ask questions to improve understanding of a text
- Predict what might happen from details stated and implied

Spoken language objectives:

- Articulate and justify answers, arguments and opinions
- Maintain attention and participate actively in collaborative conversations, staying on topic and initiating and responding to comments
- Participate in discussions, presentations, performances, role play, improvisations and debates

Curriculum links: Geography – Locational knowledge

Interest words: gazillions, fancy, swanky, forever, brow

Resources: ICT, atlases or globes

Build a context for reading

- Show children the front cover and ask them to read the title. Discuss children's ideas of why a sauce might go bang.
- Read the back cover blurb and ask children if there are any foods that they find boring. Ask children what they think might go wrong with changing the taste of food.
- Ask children to predict what might happen in the story. Encourage them to support their predictions with reasons.

Understand and apply reading strategies

- Read pp2–5 aloud, using meaning, punctuation and dialogue to help you read with expression. Discuss with the children how they can also read with expression.
- Discuss the opening of the story. How do the children feel about eating vegetables? What do they think the Special Sauce tastes like?